An Anxiety of Poets in their Natural Habitat

Amina Alyal

Stairwell Books //

Published by Stairwell Books
161 Lowther Street
York, YO31 7LZ

www.stairwellbooks.co.uk
@stairwellbooks

An Anxiety of Poets in their Natural Habitat © 2025 Amina Alyal and Stairwell Books

All rights reserved. No part of this publication may be reproduced, stored in or introduced into a retrieval system, or transmitted, in any form, or by any means (electronic, mechanical, photocopying, recording, e-book or otherwise) without the prior written permission of the author.

The moral rights of the author have been asserted.

No part of this book may be used or reproduced in any manner for the purpose of training artificial intelligence technologies or systems.

ISBN: 978-1-917334-23-5

Also by Amina Alyal

The Ordinariness of Parrots

and

Seasons of Myth - Indigo Dreams

For Molly

Table of Contents

Foreword	1
Fatuous Sunbeams	5
Eating Basho's Frog	7
In Hell or Heaven	9
Emergent poet	11
Love Poem	13
Ovidian	15
Terror Dactyls	17
Tossing Manes and Tumultuous Feet	19
Penguin Poets	21
Aftword	22
Abaftword	24

Foreword

This collection grew out of a long fascination with weird creatures in nature – the platypus, the orchid mantis, the sea-louse, the mudfish. True, a couple of more mundane creatures have found their way into these poems. But there was something about disrupting borders, about new offshoots from established categories, that was at the heart of it.

Nature does this: but do poets do it as well? Searching for a collective noun for poets, pondering on an 'unkindness of ravens' or a 'pride of lions', I came up with an 'anxiety of poets.' But this isn't a random choice. Harold Bloom, in his seminal work *An Anxiety of Influence: A Theory of Poetry*, was on my mind.[1]

Bloom argues that the 'largest truth of literary influence is that it is an inescapable anxiety: Shakespeare will not allow you to bury him, or escape him, or replace him' (xviii), and that each 'poem is a misinterpretation of a parent poem. A poem is not an overcoming of anxiety, but is that anxiety' (94). He suggests a constant striving for originality, with an inevitable connection with past poets.

---

[1] Harold Bloom, *The Anxiety of Influence*, 2nd ed. First published 1997. (Oxford University Press 1997).

But 'the anxiety of influence *comes out of* a complex act of strong misreading, a creative interpretation' (xxiii). He even asks, 'Why is influence, which might be a health, more generally an anxiety where strong poets are concerned? Do strong poets lose more, *as poets*, in their wrestling with their ghostly fathers?' (88). So while it's impossible for a poet to be a poet without reading poetry – with an intensity like 'falling in love' (xxiii) – the production of poetry verges on a struggle, an effort to create something new that is at the same time almost indivisibly a part of what came before.

Influence in postmodern terms is 'intertextuality', meaning something so much more diffuse and active than merely reading a poem and grappling with its influence – it suggests that all writing, all language, all cultural expression, is a product of fragments being drawn together, interconnected and hardly traceable. Nevertheless, I *have* traced the fragments, as best I can. These poems are intertextual, containing phrases from other poems (in italics) and you can find the references in the drawings.

Fatuous Sunbeams

I see a poet gliding through the grass,
eyes aflame with *daffodils* and *red*,
something skipping at the edge of sight,
tortoiseshell, and always just ahead.
I see a poem sliding through the glass
sweet as a beam imprinting pots of gold;
but in a moment clouds obscure the gleam,
the poet left bereft, forlorn and cold.
I see a poet swish its tail with sass,
sense dancing promises amongst the leaves
cool as a Blue Adonis – and the poet leaps –
but, claws as always void, as ever grieves.
An endless lepidopteral pursuit, alas,
awaits this poet, as others of its class.

Eating Basho's Frog

Eating this poet
is a green-sliced pickle-jar
vinegar-sharp *splash*.

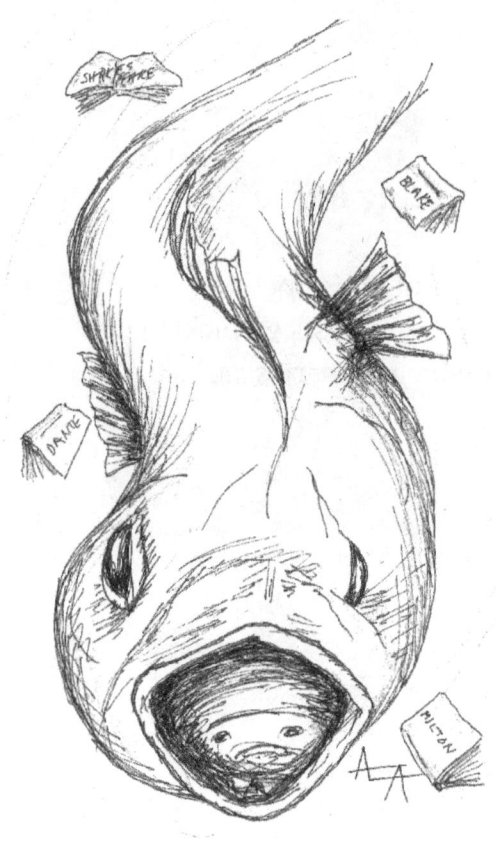

In Hell or Heaven

A tiny poet thirty fathoms down
seizes on another poet's tongue,
nel mezzo del cammin, better to reign,
reining in *the darling buds of May,*
sits itself inside the bigger poet's mouth
and guzzles blood to keep forever young.

Emergent poet

Listen, poet, listen, dark and cold:
slow, slow down.
It comes at last to cancel time.
Dry, dry utterly, deep, deep down
in *dark, cold caves.* Don't
hear thuds of feet on arid clay above
where lions hunker down in tall grasses,
or your breathing against the will
of your gills, where you slow,
slow down, a nut, an id.
You are one of the *small things;*
recoil into silence,

a mute remembrancer of crime,
long lost, concealed, forgot for years.

Wait, and there'll be an excavation
devoutly to be wish'd, a delving
when floods have slit the hills,
when *flood waters await us in our avenues,*
and waken unavailing tears,

when you'll be seen, a-swish again,
and all will say, *They existed. They existed.*

Love Poem

Petalled queen of pastel, fragile bloom,
I, poorer poet – *they call it easing the spring* –
scenting your stanza, your welcoming room,
sent to ease into your sonnet perfume

in *pretty rooms*,
a poet clad in dawn, you seem,
but
a drowsy numbness –
but you're so incisive, I didn't see
that coming, ah, *nevermore!*
If you can keep your head, keep your head, keep y –
The ocean is folded – not waving, but drowning.
This is *no country for old men.*

Ovidian

This poet is a national icon, a protected species, a velvet thing. It paddles about in gossiping waters. It is quixotic and quicksilver and was around before other poets who might think themselves immortal. It knows how to be in the shoes of poets reptilian, avian, ichthyoid, poets lutrine, poets who fly, or swim, or make dams, who give suck and who don't give birth, poets who waddle. It is master of empathy. Beware of thinking it a quaint curiosity, a fake, *a thing of patches* because, no *tim'rous beastie* this, it deals quick venom to slow down the foe.

Terror Dactyls

Here there's so many so large like a
                          bad   dream
poets who hang in the trees and then
                                        fly
made up of huge wings and *dread hands* and
                          dread   *feet,*
what should I do, put *a stake in your fat black heart?*
me in the chaos of *red*ness in *tooth* and in *claw*
seeking to *flee from* or else to devour more,
dogs eating dogs in this game of *the dogs of war.*
Bloodsucking *beast*s are these poets of *rough* maw.

Deep in the trees there's a red fluff and a
                             sweet   face,
comfort, digestible, menace all *gone with the wind,*
shape-shifting poet revealing it only eats figs.

Tossing Manes and Tumultuous Feet

You heard a poet gallop through a field
full of the fears of Spring and nothingness,
avoiding *wheelbarrows*, and toxic *daffodils*,
feeding on flesh transformed, *eating*
a *violin,* mown down by a phantom *chariot*?
You heard this galloping poet moan about
a scythe, moaning aloud?
                Were a *cloud* to be allowed
vegetable love, and *ah! bright wings,*
that poet,
      said that poet,
             might not so easily
                    startle
                          nor take
the whole field at a gallop in some vain bid.

Penguin Poets

Poets stand flipper to flipper in the cold,
ingesting far less than in days to come,
like gold to airy thinness beat
murmuring lines in the dark, singing
of sunlight lost, *song of the reed*, song
of Solomon: and how *many waters
cannot quench love*: ripples of silent
warmth pass from feather to feather

Dearth over, poets
run and skid, honking and tumbling
over each other and feasting on wine.

After the party two poets stay
side by side, watching heavenly lights
like Adam and Eve.

Aftword

As long ago as the fourteenth century, Petrarch took intertextuality for granted; there was no other way to produce poetry. What he called 'imitatio' was writing so inextricable from its predecessors that it had the resemblance of a son to a father, or a portrait to a sitter.[2] The son and the portrait, though, are new creations in their own right, and he was very aware of this. To return to Bloom, 'We need to stop thinking of a poet as an autonomous ego, however solipsistic the strongest of poets may be. Every poet is a being caught up in a dialectical relationship (transference, repetition, error, communication) with another poet or poets' (91).

But the joyously self-conscious postmodern embracing of this relationship, the collecting of scraps, the patchworking, the yoking by violence together (to rifle and misappropriate Samuel Johnson), the seepage and sponging of past materials, need not overwhelm us, as indeed Bloom recognises: 'The precursors flood us, and our imaginations can die by drowning in them, but no

---

[2] Francesco Petrarch, *Letters from Petrarch*, edited by Morris Bishop (Bloomington: Indiana University Press 1966), p. 198.

imaginative life is possible if such inundation is wholly evaded' (154). Every time we speak, we are quoting. To try not to is to miss the point.

Abaftword

Go, litel book, off with you, *galley charged with forgetfulness.* This book is the closest I'll come to an autobiography, and I leave it to readers to make what they want of it. After all, as Roland Barthes says, the author is dead as soon as the text is written, and readers then fashion it into a myriad of other internal texts, out of the networks of their own interconnections and associations. It's never the end.

Acknowledgements

'Penguin Poets' featured in Creation Theatre's production of *As You Like It* in Oxford in August 2024, where it was stuck on a tree with other poems, and appears in the gallery of a blog post about the production: https://creationtheatre.co.uk/the-modern-love-poem/

Other anthologies and collections available from Stairwell Books

First of All I Wrote Your Name	Winston Plowes
Sleeve Heart	Eleanor May Blackburn
Goldfish	Jonathan Aylett
Strike	Sarah Wimbush
Marginalia	Doreen Hinchliffe
The Estuary and the Sea	Jennifer Keevill
In | Between	Angela Arnold
Quiet Flows the Hull	Clint Wastling
Lunch on a Green Ledge	Stella Davis
there is an england	Harry Gallagher
Iconic Tattoo	Richard Harries
Herdsmenization	Ngozi Olivia Osuoha
On the Other Side of the Beach, Light	Daniel Skyle
Words from a Distance	Ed. Amina Alyal, Judi Sissons
Fractured	Shannon O'Neill
Unknown	Anna Rose James, Elizabeth Chadwick Pywell
When We Wake We Think We're Whalers from Eden	Bob Beagrie
Awakening	Richard Harries
A Stray Dog, Following	Greg Quiery
Blue Saxophone	Rosemary Palmeira
Steel Tipped Snowflakes 1	Izzy Rhiannon Jones, Becca Miles, Laura Voivodeship
Where the Hares Are	John Gilham
The Glass King	Gary Allen
Gooseberries	Val Horner
Poetry for the Newly Single 40 Something	Maria Stephenson
Northern Lights	Harry Gallagher
More Exhibitionism	Ed. Glen Taylor
The Beggars of York	Don Walls
Lodestone	Hannah Stone
Learning to Breathe	John Gilham
Throwing Mother in the Skip	William Thirsk-Gaskill
New Crops from Old Fields	Ed. Oz Hardwick
The Ordinariness of Parrots	Amina Alyal
Taking the Long Way Home	Steve Nash

For further information please contact rose@stairwellbooks.com

www.stairwellbooks.co.uk
@stairwellbooks

www.ingramcontent.com/pod-product-compliance
Lightning Source LLC
Chambersburg PA
CBHW031639160426
43196CB00006B/487